RAINBOW WISDOM
A Guide to Unlocking Your Reality Spectrum

BRAD JOHNSON

DEDICATION

This book is dedicated to all whom it may serve. Upon the Earth, we are all one family, and one united civilization. May the information contained within this book be a catalyst to those who gain expansive understandings through its contents.

TABLE OF CONTENTS

THE AUTHOR

~~~~~~

Brad Johnson

Brad Johnson began his spiritual journey in August of 2008. With the idea of creating a fascinating science fiction novel that was based around the presence of extraterrestrials and what would happen if they came upon Earth today, Brad wanted this novel to be very authentic and truthful when it came to this theme of story, so he began to do some intense research on experts, contactees and channelers to hear their viewpoints on life beyond our world. Brad's research on the extraterrestrial presence revealed some very extraordinary findings: many ETs are human in appearance, they are highly spiritual and base their existences on becoming one with an infinite creator. He also discovered that through meditation, many people are able to communicate with these beings beyond our world and receive a profound flow of consciousness-enhanced insight.

This research was astonishing to Brad and he could feel an immense transformation beginning. These discoveries caused him to begin a personal journey that started with simple meditation. Brad decided to put his novel aside and devote his focus towards a pursuit that had been lacking throughout his entire life: re-gaining his spiritual connection.

Brad began meditation by taking out a book from his local library called "Learn To Meditate: A Practical Guide to Self-Discovery and Fulfillment". Brad read this book from front to back within about 5 days. He performed many of the methods contained within the book and for the first time in his life, he began his journey into meditation. Brad's discoveries through the meditative state were astounding. He could feel his entire body reacting to the centeredness of meditation. He could feel his energy field tingling, growing, expanding, spinning, tilting as well as feel every part of his body becoming enriched with divine universal energy increasing intuitive flow.

Through his dream state, Brad was experiencing profound encounters with higher dimensional entities that were completely without any known form. He encountered what could only be explained as "non-physical classrooms" where he was being downloaded with astonishing information ranging from a variety of different topics: from the properties of oneness and universal mechanics to the understanding of self-empowerment and the creation of all life. Brad had awoken with inspiration filling his being as everything relating to the expansion of humanity and reality that was not being commonly discussed throughout popular mainstream sources.

It was through these profound discoveries that Brad decided to create an online community that comprised of psychics, intuitives, healers and metaphysical experts/seekers. Throughout this community, Brad was able to get further involved through his exploration of expanded consciousness and began to learn through many others' techniques ranging from channeling, extra sensory perception development and energy healing. Throughout the weeks that went by, Brad was developing his skill through the process of automatic writing: the ability to communicate with an extension of one's own consciousness through the mediumship of writing or drawing. Throughout many of Brad's conscious contacts with other consciousnesses via automatic writing, Brad received advice from one of his channeling mentors to direct his energy towards the star known as Sirius A, otherwise known commonly as the dog star as there was a feeling of a message that was looking to come through. Brad tuned into the energies of Sirius A and this was the first contact he had with an entity known as Adronis. Adronis began his association with Brad under the means of a soul contract. This entailed that this other consciousness extension of Brad residing from the fifth density plane of Sirius would act as a mentor for him as he worked to expand himself further through his established channeling ability.

Throughout the months ahead, Brad was able to channel Adronis further not only as a benefit to his own learning, but for the benefit of others asAdronis was willing to share his profound knowledge and inspiration with anyone who would be in resonance for contact. In the summer of 2009, Brad transcended his ability to channel from automatic writing into vocal dialogue channeling. Brad found this method to be much more convenient as it formed a personalized relationship between him, Adronis and others that were in resonance with Adronis' insightful conscious energies.

Between the years of 2009 and 2010, Brad was also expanding his knowledge in many different avenues alongside his ability to channel. In 2010, Brad founded his very own energy healing system known as Symbol Release Healing. Brad was also fascinated relating to methods that allowed him to connect directly to the Akashic records. The process was somewhat similar to the nature of channeling, and within a short period of time, Brad became very proficient at accessing energetic data from the realms of the ether within an Alpha brainwave state heightening advanced processing functions.

Throughout the upcoming years, Brad was offered to join several seminars and conferences along the west coast of North America: from his local area of Vancouver, BC, Canada to Seattle, Washington, Portland, Oregon and many regions across the state of California. Throughout the span of December of 2009 to the approaching end of 2012, Adronis has shared a vast degree of knowledge and wisdom through Brad regarding a broad range of subject matter: personal and professional transformation, self empowerment, personal healing, history of mankind, our Earth, galaxy and universe, ET contact and disclosure, the power of paradox, evolution past polarity & much more.

Throughout Brad's ability to strengthen his connection as a conduit functioning as an ally of universal knowledge, Brad had reached the point where he is able to consciously connect to his own soul matrix and retrieve specific subject matter. This ability has been termed by Brad as Conscious Matrix Communication: the very basis for the understanding of Rainbow Wisdom.

In December of 2012, Brad introduced his newest energy healing concept that was developed through his connection of Conscious Matrix Communication. This newest healing system known as Light Circuitry Atunement: *(formerly known as Body Regeneration Healing)* the ability to work through one's soul matrix utilizing holograms and one's own natural intuitive state to repair the body and purify the flow of energy through the means of harmonized "4-D healing".

Brad has mentioned on many occasions that there is really nothing special about what he does. It is an ability that everyone has access to. Whether one wishes to become a channeler or a conscious matrix communicator, it's all within our grasp. All it requires is the commitment to live all elements of what such a lifestyle represents. We are all gifted in our own ways and will express our gifts in the themes that best suit us. Brad's job has always been to awaken, inspire and expand, and this is what he aims for with dedication through every person he interacts with.

INTRODUCTION

What is Rainbow Wisdom?

Just as one would look upon a rainbow and be in awe of its beauty through the array of colors within its structure, one who holds Rainbow Wisdom can see the beauty of the array of understanding within their own self structure.

To be a being of Rainbow Wisdom far surpasses the idea of knowing their self. On the contrary, the premise is that one who has travelled through their facets of knowing to transcend it to unknowing is well on their way to becoming one of Rainbow Wisdom. Your destiny consciousness is meant to be as broad and expansive as your essence beyond the body. The Rainbow Wise understand that all themes of life exist to be completed so that transcendence can be acclaimed.

13

The transcendence is far more than being a self-empowered individual. Self-empowerment will certainly grant a profound achievement relating to stretching your boundaries and even dissolving them. But transcendence promotes the way of unlearning to return to a vessel of purity. One who does not hesitate to follow the impulses of their heart. One who loves and listens to him or herself and becomes the pure vibration of service. There are no hesitations, conflicts, doubts, disbeliefs, grief nor fear. All that exists is the one moment. Here and now becomes your entirety.

One of Rainbow Wisdom is that of a courageous soul who dives deeply into the contrast of their own matrix. They do not escape nor ignore pain; they acknowledge it and thank it for being there. Pain exists to explore its infrastructure so that re-alignment can be attracted.

The colours of the rainbow holds an immense spectrum, as does the nature of our pain and programming. It is a collection of unique distortions representing limitation and self-unworthiness. Intricately designed in many avenues that holds fail safes when the beginning of transcendence commences. The programming we carry does not give up with a very intense fight.

Additionally, it encourages you to fight back against it so that you can only imagine you are leaving one box to find yourself contained within another. As long as defiance through resistance exists, you will not achieve transcendence. You will only continue to dance through a vast maze of programmed distortion keeping you against walls that will seem unbreakable.

The Rainbow Wise understand that the three most powerful words of their essence are "I love you." These are the words that transcend walls and advance past the maze of programmed distortion. If you already can say these three words to yourself as you look into the mirror without feeling any effect of unworthiness, you are already beginning your illuminating journey as the Rainbow Wise.

This book does not teach you, nor does it insist anything upon you. It is only here to remind you. The Rainbow Wise simply exist as a prism to relay your light on both ends of the spectrum: the rainbow light flowing through the prism to return as the white light of Source, and the white light flowing through the prism to share in its creation distortion to grant the gift of experience. The Rainbow Wise bless the distortion that has cast the hologram of experience throughout this universe as it is the depth of ourselves exploring the endless facets of our inner creation. The Rainbow Wise also bless the distortion looking to become one again with Source consciousness and serve in reflection as catalyst to become transcendence.

This book shares the philosophy of unlearning and transcending the boundaries of distortion aligning you to the natural one. It shall not do it for you, but it can assist in you helping yourself to become the full spectrum of the rainbow reality. All enlightenment is through the one. All realization of distortion is through the one. Your journey from self to all to one—is through the one. You are about to embark upon an illuminating self-journey, dear reader. May it be well in serving your unlearning and transcendence.

With love and appreciation,

Brad Johnson

CHAPTER 1

Being an Ego Ally

Through many variations of material found throughout the world, it is not uncommon to find others sharing their story relating to 'getting past' the ego so that one can experience enlightenment. There have been techniques shared on how one is able to escape or kill their ego so that a state of self-empowerment and tranquility can be achieved.

Let us be mindful that the ego itself is not meant to be destroyed, assassinated, blown up, vaporized, nuked, run from, ignored or killed. It is of the Rainbow Wise to see your ego as a companion. The ego will be with you your entire life from the day that you are born until the day that you retire from the physical body. The ego has been sophisticated in its design to serve originally as a device to maintain continuity through your living reality so that you may interface with experience. The ego exists as a memory tool on a physical, mental and emotional level. It learns, grows, adapts and maintains memory-based coding that adds to the compliment of one's own lifestyle—through its original design.

In this book, you will not see that the distortion of unnatural experiences are labeled as a result of 'ego.' Unnatural experience is used as a term representing what has been received through the ego as memory leading to assignment that has generated imbalance within one's own life. This helps to provide a broader perspective in understanding why the ego has been belittled as the culprit to our own inadequacies.

First of all, it is for you to realize that the ego is not and has never been an enemy. The memory capability it contains through its construction has been subjected to the basis of programming ever since the day you have been born. After all, with many of us, the first thing we do when we are born is cry as we leave a womb of tranquility and afloat stillness only to be brought into a world where the thoughts and actions of the people in our environment portray an overwhelming amount of confusion and belief.

When we are young, our ego ally is learning alongside us so that we can attain continuity through memory to become familiar on how we can exist within our environment. It is through the ego that you are able to walk, sit, talk, eat, learn, memorize and perform particular skills and talents. Your ego is complimenting your comforts of daily life performing what we could consider to be natural processes. The ego is absolutely adept in remembering, memorizing and adapting. It is its greatest trait.

So, if the ego is originally such an adept grounding device, why have we been so compelled to accuse ourselves or others of "egos" when we see discomfort? The situation does not represent the doing of the ego on its own, but the undisciplined state of maturity for us as children moving into adulthood. We lack in the necessary discernment skills to fully understand what type of distorted unnatural experiences are entering our minds and being absorbed by the ego as memory. The issue comes not from the ego, but from the distorted programs operating within our reality to become repetitive so that our ego is susceptible to attaining these learning distortions through its memory matrix. As the distortions are constantly in a state of repeat through what is known as morality, ethics, values and education; we become acclimatized to these repetitions so that they can feel natural to our ego. Through it, this is memory; and it is its duty to maintain the continuity with what has been assigned as learning within our reality.

When there is deviation from the memory contained within the ego, there is great resistance that emerges. The ego will utilize aspects of your own subconscious to attempt to correct the 'error' of you deviating from a path of ego memory. It is not because the ego is feeling betrayed and is personally offended by you, it is because its design is not being recognized and it cannot fathom the act of deviation without adequate memory to serve as a counter-balance to a belief system it still considers to be valid. This is why when individuals who are suffering are told they have the capability to walk another life path and improve their personal growth, career and financial areas; they become frustrated and highly skeptical. There is no valid experience of memory through the ego that would warrant the confirmation of such a statement. The ego cannot 'imagine' whatsoever.

That is an ability through our own natural state of being. It is only a memory database that stores data representing how you have lived your life. What is happening in this now moment is foreign to the ego and considered illogical for it to process.

Are you now seeing the misconception when one blames their own ego or the ego of another due to personal discomfort? The issue has never been abolishing the ego, but forming a strong alliance with it so that you can assist in its re-programming and unlearning. Our systems and way of life are the very essences that have caused the ego to become inflated with bloated distortion. Similar to how computers may have malware within them, our common beliefs, values, morality and ethics are the very malware for our own ego that has caused it to become distorted with unnatural experiences.

How Does the Alliance Begin?

When one has reached the realization to alter their life's path, the first thing begins with looking into your own self-value. Self-value that becomes encouraged, believed and housed as a natural program within the ego will allow one to live a life complimentary to that form.

As stated in the Introduction, one who is of the Rainbow Wise understands the three powerful words that is the heart of their essence: "I love you." This would be a recommended first step for those who are looking to ally with their own ego.

If one has trouble saying "I love you" while looking into their own eyes through a mirror, there can be no alliance between their own natural being and their own ego as they do not believe nor feel worthy of the love that they speak to themselves. The Rainbow Wise live their lives through the essence of love that exists enriched within their hearts. Without the love, you will be at the mercy of programs, systems and thought forms that will continue to distort your ego creating further self-impairment.

Have you said "I love you" to yourself today? If you haven't, it is recommended that you place this book down, walk in front of a mirror, look into your eyes and see yourself speaking the words "I love you" aloud. The very reaction of these three words is felt to the very core of your being.

For those who are not accustomed to saying this to themselves on a daily basis, this will seem awkward and even foreign. It may take some time before you have gained enough confidence to naturally say this to yourself in the mirror each day. But each time that you feel compelled to say these words to your own mirror reflection, it will become part of a new harmonized ego program. In fact, you may notice that as you do this more, your ego will actually remind you to perform this action as it becomes accustomed to the program. This is the very reason why this is performed on a daily basis: you are re-programming the ego with positive reinforcement to counter-balance environmentally unnatural programming.

Can you imagine creating your own ego as a reflection of your physical self? Can you also imagine sitting down at a table with your physicalized ego and going over aspects of your life that are now looking to be acknowledged, forgiven and liberated? This is another recommended exercise that can allow you to bring your natural self and your ego to the same level. You are going into a reflection period together evaluating and acknowledging the belief systems that are still contained within the ego. This is the first step in achieving ego and natural alliance.

If you have struggled with finances, career, relationships, etc., bring them out before your ego. Imagine that they are folders placed on the table, opened up and observed. Note the ego's concerns as it feels that the belief system must remain as there is no remedy to these situations. This is where the imagination begins to take form creating a positive reinforcement that will allow a course of action to be conceived. Explain to your ego that you will bring positive reinforcement to this belief system so that it can be illuminated and transcended past distortion. Reach an agreement with your ego and work together to attain memory on performing a positively reinforced experience. Just like you are working to say "I love you" in the mirror every day, let repetition serve you in aligning to this positive event. As you do this more and more, the ego will be allied with you and will work together with you for a common cause: manifesting new positive programming.

The Ability to Forgive & Encountering Energy Vampires

Whereas it may seem simple, this is one of the most challenging traits to administer. With the trauma of many belief systems that have been attached to the ego, the ability to wipe the slate clean is foreign to your ally. Positive reinforcement is the genesis to beginning the path of forgiveness. You will begin to understand that all hardships and traumas have existed in order for us to improve upon ourselves. Our lives are messy with a great deal of turmoil that stains our souls since childhood. The turmoil will need to be addressed and forgiven if we ever intend to transcend ourselves. No matter the trauma, no matter the hardship, the bravest and most illuminating beings are the ones that still have the courage to forgive themselves and others. Extreme situations were experienced through us as a way of reminding us who we really are within by first showing us who we aren't without. As long as we had continued to fight going against the grain and living through unnatural distortion, the extremes would only become more severe. It would be no different than having tar poured upon you, then having yourself volunteer to pour more hot tar upon yourself and then rolling into an enormous lake filled with tar drenching yourself in it. This would require a strong reinforcement to cleanse yourself of the sticky, sickening tar and its noxious fumes. As long as we continue to ignore who we truly are and what we are within, those buckets of thick, black tar will only continue to be voluntarily dumped upon us.

To hold grudges through ourselves and others has become quite simple through our societal indoctrination. To point a finger and blame is easy.

To destroy one's own confidence and not attempt a path of greatness takes no effort whatsoever. Criticizing, judging and ridiculing are by far the easiest response because such mentality is based out of an individual who feels helpless, hopeless and inferior within themselves. They do not see their inner greatness, and so they give up on their dreams and passions. They are vibrating at the level of a victim consciousness feeling that if they don't deserve empowerment, no one else does and they will make it their work to bring as many people to their level as they can. These individuals are often known throughout society as "energy vampires." Yet, it is important to realize that they are not draining your energy per se, they simply emit frequencies of intense emotional thought that hold a powerful magnetism to those who think differently. As their emotional states are high, they hold a great deal of dramatic influence. One who has still not come to peace with their own dramatic cycles can be influenced profoundly by these individuals that project powerful thought forms of emotional states. The only way one is influenced through themselves when meeting these particular individuals is that there is a relationship formed through mutual insecurity. When that happens, the energy vampire has succeeded in bringing you to their vibratory level of intense emotional drama. You will then begin to feel as they do: highly judgmental and powerless against their own states of emotional turmoil.

When faced with such individuals who are intent on bringing you to their level, send them love and learn to walk away from it. You cannot help these individuals as a catalyst because they are unwilling to be helped at this time. Right now, they want to be superiority by showing you their mentality bred by inferiority. It is what's known as a 'no-win situation.' Love them as they are a spark of the divine just as you, only they are lost within the fog that they have cast upon themselves. Let them be and depart from their company in peace. It is not about retaliation, it is about recognition and realizing when one cannot be assisted only at this time.

It is through this example of the energy vampire that forgiveness is the greatest tool within you. As judgment, criticism and ridicule are so easy to project within society, your true courage will come from how much you still love a person regardless of the fog cast around them. When you can see the divine within them and see them as part of you, regardless if you are unable to assist them or not, then you have gained a greatness within yourself. One may spew a large amount of emotional tar upon you, but when you are not affected by their dramatic influences as you have transcended your own, your energy will be untouchable and unbendable when it comes to dramatic emotional onslaught. See the divine, feel the divine and be the divine. By becoming this mentality, you will be part of an incredible self-reality that will provide you with enlightening experience far beyond anything the imagination can conceive of. It is through this that forgiveness can grant if you truly see its effectiveness as a natural tool to liberation.

The Ego and Natural Self as One

Can you imagine waking up every morning and having your own ego encourage you to perform positive actions that will make your day an illuminating one? This is a very real possibility. After all, this was the original intention of the ego: it exists to compliment your reality through memory as you attract compliment through yourself. This is the path where you natural self and the ego are one. Your naturalness brings you into new heights of awareness and enlightenment and your ego paves the path to experience these effects through the interface of continuity-based reality. Your life feels like it is the most beautiful dream you can imagine. You are no longer tethered to the demands of what society has expected from you. You are now unbounded exploring your world through the connections of enlightenment that enrich your mind, body and spirit.

The key to this tranquility doesn't involve attempting to normalize yourself so that you are socially accepted into the whole. Rather, you are integrating society within yourself so that your interpretation of it feels whole. Society is known as the collective ego of humanity. Where it has the potential to be as supportive and encouraging as your own ego once it is aligned to your compliment, it exists as a flurry of unnatural distortion as it still does not understand itself as a whole. It is fragmented and going through an intense state of collective duality. More important than that, however; it is beyond your ability to repair. Society can only be repaired through society itself starting with each individual that harmonizes and allies with their own ego just as you can. Do not feel that you must limit yourself to the insecurity that the societal collective is experiencing. Take the aspects of what you appreciate regarding the idea of society and let that be your own personal integration. Be who you feel would be a prime example of a member of society as you exist in compliment and alliance with your ego and your natural self. It is through this amalgamation effect that you're able to experience liberation and boundless opportunity as an illuminating being walking their inner path of Rainbow Wisdom.

CHAPTER 2

Attracting & Managing Thought

Throughout all of creation, there is but one law that exists: the law of one. All expressions, experiences, realities, dimensions, causalities and thoughts are one. Thought represents a creative dynamic distortion instituted through the holographic universe of experience. When we project the white light of Source through the prism of experience, the effect creates the rainbow light distortion as filters of unbridled possibility consisting of experiential exploration are present.

Thought simply represents meaning. For one to become inspired, accomplish a venture and to reflect, thought is required. It is a dynamic not created by an individual, but a coded pattern of information created through consciousness as a prop to a dynamically created universe birthing a gift of experience through the one that magnetizes him or herself to its property.

No one has ever created an original thought. As thoughts are universal dynamics adaptable to an experiencer, they have become symbiotic to an infinitum of hosts throughout the universe. Similar to how we understand that the measurements of the natural universe exists through the program of fractal geometry, thoughts are also fractal in their creative essence: they have no owner and are the property of not one being within all of creation.

Our human bodily vessels exist as perception devices remotely piloted through non-localized consciousness. Our non-localized consciousness is the stream to where the cluster of thoughts associative to our personality archetypes flow through our bodies to provide us with the ability of themed experience.

This is why many of us are able to identify with certain mystical systems that help to understand our own archetypal themes: astrology, numerology, etc. Where we are born on the planet, our time of birth, the phase of the moon and the alignments of the planets during our birthing are synchronic algorithms that function as personality programs. This enables the theme of our non-localized consciousness' choosing to become birthed through incarnation functioning as the person we are today. Our thoughts are the result of our own themed-based programming that have already been appropriated through consciousness existing beyond space, time and matter.

Managing Thoughts

Although one cannot create an original thought, one can certainly perceive an original thought: these would be known as pure thoughts or pure thinking. Pure thinking involves a consortium of thoughts that are not represented through the archetype through pre-conceived systems generated by archaic thought implementation. One who is Rainbow Wise is a vessel to share in a pure thought process. The pure thought is unique to the individual and initiates a course of action through the thought to generate an authentic experience from the thought perceiver. This would also be known as the "Inception state."

The generation of a pure thought comes from the dismantling of archaic thought paradigms. The thought that initiates an idea off the basis of pre-conceived notions that denotes expansion is the result of an archaic or doctrinal thought. These thoughts are limiting and do not encourage expansion. At their prime level, they are stepping-stone thoughts only existing to be surpassed so that advancement can be achieved with the archaic thought functioning as a predecessor leading to pure thought.

For example, when one experiences a brief moment of the Inception state, or otherwise known as an "A-ha!" moment, this is an example of a pure thought. It was a thought that was granted to the perceiver in a moment of un-expectancy. A pure thought can never be searched for, it can only be perceived when one is in the appropriate vibratory frequency to receive it. Many that have had "A-ha!" moments had allowed their mind to be free of the question or pondering. Their daily life had continued as usual and later on in the day, by being observant of environmental stimuli or 'triggers' contained within reality, the Inception state is aligned and the "A-ha!" moment becomes perceived.

It is possible to have many of these "A-ha!" moments within a single day. The key is to not expect the purity of thought and to allow your mind to be free of burdening archaic thoughts that illicit distraction from the now moment. When you are as close to unthinking as possible, you are the most prone to inspiration.

Think of a cluttered mind as a cluttered room filled with many guests. Within this room is a pure thought. But you cannot allow yourself to be visited by the pure thought as the archaic thoughts are constantly surrounding you all speaking to you simultaneously with enormous voices. As you clear your mind and let those archaic thoughts float by not attaching to your attention, the thoughts pass through you like an apparition and you are able to be at peace within your own room. While you are at peace, at the appropriate timing, a pure thought has the opportunity to visit you as long as it serves in your endeavoring to be of natural self-service.

Entangled Within Belief

When one believes in something, it does not represent a state of natural confidence. Belief simply holds one's own faith towards an idea. A belief is something that is faithful through assumption, yet not experienced for it to become naturalness within one's own self. Yet, when one holds a belief, a great deal of the value pertaining to that belief is extremely powerful. Like the idea of faith, belief becomes a personal religion to an individual as it represents an identity of attached value. It is a compensation that holds together the identity bridge as the individual does not trust themselves to look deeper past the belief. Therefore, expansion can never visit one who is deeply emerged in belief. The belief(s) govern the archetype of thoughts within its themes limiting any form of pure thought to enter the mainframe of the individual's mind complex.

How can one overcome belief? The same as when an alcoholic consciously decides to stop drinking or to stop taking drugs. It must be realized so that the individual no longer craves the addiction for such a belief. The moment the belief no longer holds any personal value to the individual, it becomes liberated. The greatest healer that has ever existed has been and always will be yourself. Others can always be of assistance and may offer profound insight to you. But if you are not in the alignment to receive insight through such catalysts representing family, friends, professionals, etc., then the insight will provide no personal comfort or liberation as you are not in sync on a vibratory level for realization to visit you. There is no magic formula that works for everyone when it comes to personal healing. There is only your magic formula, and when you discover it through your own trials of attempting to transcend beliefs, the process will become much more illuminating as you learn from what you are able to liberate through you mind, body and spirit pertaining to belief.

What you can do is provide rhetorical stimulating questions to lead you into further acknowledgement of the beliefs you carry. Only you can look deeper through these questions to help you understand your personal attachment to such beliefs that deliver such thoughts that make you feel devoted to the systems in your mind:

> *Do I remember when this belief first came to me?*
>
> *Why do I hold this belief system in such high regard? What is its value?*
>
> *Does this belief encourage my personal feeling of liberation? Do I feel boundless and free through it? Why or why not?*
>
> *If I were able to un-assign this belief from my being, how do I think I would feel without it?*

As previously discussed, the belief system must be addressed In alliance with your own ego.

Come together and evaluate the belief system(s) together through these questions above.

Stimulating Positive Thoughts

Although the specific technique for positive thought stimulation is subjectively-based, the collective performance to stimulate positive thoughts has led to a very high success rate in the dissolving of belief systems. If the one is committed enough to transcending their beliefs through the love and naturalness of Rainbow Wisdom, more systems suppressing the invitation of pure thoughts will become far more prominent.

As a creator, you deserve all of the love within creation. The seduction, however; of physical reality attempts to entrap us into believing we are limited beings incapable of living a life of joy, love and expansion. It is time to begin bringing in the stimulation of positive thoughts by learning to understand what you are deserving of.

A list of positive thoughts and actions can be a mile long, but if you don't feel you deserve to experience any of those criteria written on your list, you will not attract them.

It is for you to understand that you are a magnet that attracts particular thoughts through your own assigned beliefs. To re-define yourself and question those beliefs allows new thought forms to enter your mind encouraging stimulation. To allow the beliefs to fully dissolve, however; you will need to be in touch with what you feel you naturally deserve:

You deserve to live a healthy and productive lifestyle.

You deserve to be in a career that you are truly excited in exploring.

You deserve to have a strong inner circle of people who are a manifested compliment to you.

You deserve to become financially abundant.

You deserve to become the person that lives a life of joy every single day.

How do you feel when you read those deserving statements? How would you feel if all of those statements came true within your life? This is the process to managing your thoughts based upon your deserving aims in life. Look into your strengths and focus upon them. Create stimuli that will inspire and encourage you to bring positive, authentic thoughts into your mind that brings you into thinking in a way you have never have before.

- Create a vision board filled with images of positive influence.

- Write in a journal or blog to share ideas with yourself that encourage positive thinking.

- Be aware of belief-based thoughts. Acknowledge that they exist and create a reflection of positive solution that will grant them liberation from your body, mind and spirit.

When managing your thoughts, it Is not about documenting every single thought that you have each day, but be mindful of how you feel on a daily basis. What feelings did you experience today? How would you rate your day on a scale of 1 to 10? What can you do to make your day tomorrow a perfect 10?

Constantly stimulate your mind with positive thinking. Again, we are re-programming the distortions of unnatural experiences through the ego so that you are primed to thinking in a balanced, natural way. As you continue to stimulate unnatural experience with positive reinforcement, you will eventually feel those situations returning to a point of balanced harmony. You will no longer feel the definitions of the negative or the positive. They will simply become what is: devoid of meaning and neutralized into true liberation.

When a great majority of your being is transcended into the alignment of neutralized liberation, you are becoming stronger with the flow of Rainbow Wisdom.

All Thoughts Are Borrowed

Like your body, mind and spirit, all energy that exists within the universe is borrowed. All that you are is part of the universe in ways you can't even imagine. Thought is no different.

We as humans feel that we need to attain a feeling of property or ownership with what we experience: "These are my feelings through my mind and my body." No, they are not.

You are borrowing the sensation of feeling to interpret the borrowed thoughts that are flowing through your borrowed universal mind experienced through your borrowed body created of the Earth, the galaxy and the universe. There is and never has been anything that you have ever owned. Ownership is nothing more than the product of a belief created through the illusion of programming-based identity.

Thoughts exist abundantly throughout our universe in different dimensions and realities. They are summoned to use through the natural vibratory frequency that we are broadcasting through ourselves. We experience them because we are in relationship with them. We are sharing the same plane where co-creatorship grants the expression of thought to emerge with feeling defined with meaning through the heart of man.

The Rainbow Wise are able to form a relationship with thought as a host would welcome a traveling visitor. The host knows that the visitor's stay is temporary and when the visitor has fulfilled their welcome, they will depart from the company of the host in love, respect and appreciation. This is the very nature of the relationship representing thought: You are the host and the thought is the visitor. It flows through you until its essence of experience is fulfilled and is then able to depart from you without attachment. You were thankful for its presence as it brought experience representing its matrix to you. The thought can now return to the universe for another host to be enriched by its experiential essence. May it go in peace and may the thought become ever-expansive through its infinite visits with an endless amount of hosts. That is the understanding with the nature of its relationship.

Feel the thought like a wave of water rushing from a river. It will pass through you like a stone on the riverbed never attaching or feeling owned by the stone. Only a brief encounter exists between the stone and the rushing wave of water. Thought is meant to stream. You are meant to interface with a prolific amount of experiences that affect all areas of your life. That is the nature of living—it is the nature of existing.

CHAPTER 3

Manifestation Mechanics

Within this reality, our manifestations are not singular-based, but collective-based. Manifestations are not instantaneously received the moment that we think about them. In a way, this can be quite a relief for a mind that is not disciplined enough to feel that their thoughts operate through them on a level of guidance. If an undisciplined mind unable to manage their thoughts was granted instant manifestation, it would be safe to say that many of us would most likely end up destroying ourselves, others and the entire planet.

Our manifestations are filtered through the current arrangement of alignment pertaining to our Earth, our moon and our planets. They are a harmonic convergence keeping instant thought manifestations at bay. Geometrical alignments formed by the planetary harmonic grid creates a certain fractal energy algorithm that allows each of us to operate on a cooperative collective level when it comes to thought streams. Not only that, but there are higher forms of consciousness that exist as caretakers who assist in the management of collective thought forms that are appropriated for our current level of human maturity development. These managerial conscious beings existing in non-physical planes would exist within the area that we would understand as our own Van Allen radiation belt. Within the vicinity of this belt also houses the Earth experiment of souls that are 'queued' to incarnate upon our world as living beings.

As we cannot singularly manifest through material, we can manifest through perception, and it is in this chapter where you will be taken on a tour on how you can play within the harmony of your perceptual reality: you will understand how one can exist fully in compliment with their experiences, catalysts and perceptive manifestations.

Reality is by Interpretation

When you look at the basis of reality, we are all looking at a picture of an abstract pattern. This pattern continues to change and shift its appearance within every frame of motion within existence. When looking at this abstract pattern, there is no certainty, there is only perspective. There is no answer, there is only truth. This is how the universe is meant to be perceived: it is a continuum of dynamic creations observable and perceived by the one functioning as infinite vantage points through the all. This very universal dynamic function serves under the one law—the law of one. It is all of creation looking within itself through an infinitum of distorted vantage points orchestrated through now and forever that mirror the whole of the one.

Why is this important to understand? Simply because there is never a wrongness existing through the one law. Wrongness is a perspective seen through the distortion of judgment that stems through the distortion of a vantage point. There has never been a polarity assigned to the events, circumstances and decisions in your life other than the ones that you have deemed to be self-valid. You exist on this planet because it is a perspective of illusory separation that gifts the greatest potential for purified unity consciousness. All other reasons, credence or clarifications are simply self-imposed through your own perspective of self and others.

Therefore, as we know we are part of the infinite whole, our perspectives exist no differently than a gear among an infinite menagerie of gears. It is not about the colour of the gear, or the type of gear, but only that the gear continues to move in symmetry with the corresponding gears so that the cycle of life creation continues to prosper so that the universal dynamic flows harmoniously. A gear can never be disrupted in its direction of motion, nor can it be removed from the infinite system.

No matter the direction of your choosing in life, you will always be in existence to serve the flow of the infinite. Even in our darkest days, it exists as the cyclic plan for a gear to transform itself into a further stabilizing gear that responds in kind to the momentum of harmonious movement: synchronized and aligned still a part of the perfection of cyclic harmony throughout the infinite creation. The self cannot outthink, out-determine or out-perceive spirit as the self is nothing more than a device housed and operated by spirit. So, in summary, there is nothing you can do in life that will ever go against the flow of what you know to be divine. All is part of the plan. All is harmony. All is one.

Choice is the Magnetic of Momentum

The actions we embark upon selected through choice is part of a momentum current that takes you upon a powerfully-charged path generated through your state of being in that moment. When you are disharmonized with unnatural programing, your state of being will produce momentum currents to choose elements proficient to that misalignment. This is what's known as 'going against the grain.' Nonetheless, no being ever stays on that path forever. It is a burdening path felt through the self, and one can only take so much of unnatural selection through the momentum current of choice. There will come a point where realization grants you the momentum upon the true path of your nature: the path of harmony. Everyone will get to this point as it is inevitable. Only each of us will get to that point in our own adequate timing; regardless if it may take years or lifetimes.

Every Manifestation is a Collective Manifestation

With every intention we place through ourselves to be cycled through the universe and propagated through feedback, all manifestations that occur in this reality serve the alignment and allotment of the collective whole. There is no such thing as an independent manifestation as that holds illusory discord. All life is one and so all life must reciprocate into appropriate conjunctions of relating energies for one's intention to become propagated as perceived manifestation through the whole.

Think of it similar to an audition process. One who wishes to be incredibly wealthy by feeling they can win the lottery will very rarely receive such a manifestation for a variety of reasons. There is no part in the collective whole at this time for that particular individual to win a wealth of fortune through such a configuration of numerical randomness. One would be mindful if they began to explore a vaster opportunistic approach should they decide to follow a path of great financial wealth. This begins with the individual aligning to the course of their own value when it comes to financial matters. You are creating an energetic resume as it were. You are intending to follow a path that holds a numerous amount of opportunities on how you wish to become financially wealthy. As you pose this manifestation request through perspective, the universe will process your intent similar to an administrator. Days may pass and the universe is now presenting you with new opportunities that are in relationship to your request: new career openings and new people to appear within your reality leading you to this request of financial abundance.

The challenge, however; is being mindful of the opportunities that come before you. Many of us only decide to go for opportunities that seem obvious to our intended manifestation and leave all other avenues behind in the dark. Let yourself feel out every opportunity that comes your way just as if you were imagining dipping your toe in many ponds to determine which pond felt the most comforting to you.

With any of the choices you make, remember that your intention will lead you into a co-creation. We are a co-creative planet and any manifestation you feel you can think of will always correspond in relationship to other people, environments and circumstances that all resonate together. It is the gear turning so that the other gears can correspond in unified harmony to turn in symmetry with the cyclic movement.

Living Life through Invitation

The Rainbow Wise understands that the greatest compliment to their reality involves adjusting their life's inner circle with people, thoughts and circumstances of the highest possible harmonic preference. When you attract those that are in harmony with your life in all forms imaginable, your life becomes a manifestation dreamland: your passions will grow, your health will improve, your life attributes on all levels will seem surreal as you experience reality in a way you never thought possible!

How does one of the Rainbow Wise invite in such compliment, and what is meant by the inner circle? Compliment can only be achieved from one who has been through the experience to understand that change on a higher level is the only way to lead to a personal ascension in life. In other words, one who has experienced intense turmoil through all the themes of their reality now has the wisdom to grow from them. The key to this is self-admittance. As discussed earlier, you are befriending your ego and allying with vulnerability. When you do this, the vulnerability becomes acknowledged, accepted, forgiven and liberated. Now you become aligned to your vibration of compliment as that is the result of befriending vulnerability and assigning the ego as an ally.

Your inner circle relates to the 'major roles' of players that exist within your life: family, friends, co-workers, teachers, etc. These are the people who have been with you for a long time and hold a strong impact with your level of relationship. The more complimentary the major players are within your life as well as the more influence you are receiving that represents positive reinforcement, support and love; the more your thoughts become harmonized to such an influence based on your environment. It Is through this harmonic influence that function in tandem with your harmonized ego which brings you into a strong inner circle relationship. It is the foundation of your reality as all major players, thoughts and resulting reflecting circumstances manifest exist within the forefront of your reality.

Ask yourself these questions to begin developing the compliment of your inner circle:

- Do I feel supported within my life in this very moment?

- Do I feel that all major players within my life are a compliment to my inner circle of reality relationship?

- Do I feel I have learned all I can from those who may feel conflicting to my personal evolution, and am I now discerning enough to decide who to invite as well as who to un-invite into my reality?

Uninviting the Old Major Players

One may feel that their family members, for example; may be very conflicting to their personal evolution. This is certainly understandable as well as very commonplace. What does one do if they feel they are being held under a veil of influence from a family member or close friend?

It is for you to understand that no matter the alignment of the major player, you are only living through one intimate life on this planet, and that is your own. Just as you would respect the space, decisions and freedoms of another, those very notions are meant to be complimented to you just the same. Many people are still very much programmed through belief that you must live a certain way according to their expectations. Should you deviate that, their actions would be to bombard you in any form that would attempt to generate guilt and shame through you. It is these very tactics that are the programming of an energy vampire as discussed earlier.

Remember that no matter who the major player is, what you are looking to build is a reality of deep compliment. This may involve you being very discerning with who you decide to continue to interact with through your current configuration of your inner circle. These discernments can be quite challenging, but if they are not dealt with out of respect and value for yourself, the conflict will only continue to escalate as your awareness is now primed for higher learning.

This is what can cause others to look for 'escapes' within their reality. They understand that they are interacting with other major players that do not represent compliment to the inner circle, and so they must look to an extreme that involves numbing themselves while their reality is configured within chaos. No action is taken in inviting those in who are a compliment to the inner circle and so the individual's reality becomes further traumatizing generating victim consciousness and helplessness.

As it is meant to be known, only the one Is capable of changing themselves. It cannot be done by anyone else within your reality. You will need to be the one who decides, discerns and releases those who you feel conflict with your reality so that substitution leading to invitation can proceed. Let the guidance provided in this book be a tool for you, but the course of action you decide to pursue must be made by you and only you.

The Invitation Process

How can one invite in complimentary major players into their inner circle? The answer as it follow manifestation mechanics is that you must become the compliment yourself. As you see the strengths of who you are beyond the weaknesses, you give yourself a new ground to explore.

For example, if you feel some of your strengths represents that of a good listener and a natural leader, let your reality reflect in that complement of being a good listener and a natural leader. This can involve attending social gatherings that you have personal interest in and becoming the example of a good listener and natural leader. As you know these to be your strengths without any doubt, reality will correspond to that manifestation mechanic. One that holds true to their strengths will gain greater imminence in restructuring their inner circle with compliment. Manifestation operates at a quick pace when you are more in alliance to your natural knowing. This idea transcends belief as you no longer 'think' that you are a natural leader, you 'know' that you are a natural leader.

The holographic universe is simply that. Physical reality is the result of a hologram susceptible to be contorted through form by a purely focused mind generated by true intent. If your true intent is an attribute such as leadership, you will attract in kind the holograms that are appropriate to that thought. Like attracts like. You are simply surrounded by mirrors of yourself in every moment. Why not cast the most profound reflections to explore the depths of your greatness through what you naturally prefer? You can do this as you have already experienced reality through what you haven't preferred. As you understand this property of manifestation mechanic and reaffirm your inner circle in such compliment, you venture further into the harmony of Rainbow Wisdom.

CHAPTER 4

Enhancing Intuitive Ability

As a civilization, we have greatly forgotten what it is to think from a place from the heart. The convoluted mechanism that we have been so heavily bred into has been the mechanism of logic.

Intuition holds the most natural energy within our entire being. Logic is not intended as a natural energy that compliments simplicity. To imply logic in such a way is to exist in life with a skewed perspective that's in antithesis to how we can evolve as a creator.

Logic is not meant to be cast aside, but it Is not meant to be embraced as the primary tool in understanding the self, others and the reality spectrum. Logic is a device of grounding. It assists in anchoring the experience of causality so that our interface within such a realm can become a possibility.

What is also important to understand is that logic is incapable of ideas. Ideas are the result of intuitive feeling. Logic is the pattern of manifestation that helps to bring the energies of the idea into physical reality. You can liken the idea of intuition as an artist and logic is the paintbrush ready to paint upon the canvas of reality. Without the artist, the canvas will not paint itself. The true beauty of the art in its totality comes from the feeling of the painter with logic only complimenting his expression through the stroke of the brush decided by intuition.

Being Intuitive and Becoming Psychic

What is the difference between intuition and psychic ability? Intuition would be considered as a sixth sense that naturally exists through the awareness of our body. The "gut feeling" or "flutters" within the heart or the "butterflies" in the stomach all represent sensations of intuition. It is our body's natural reaction to the state of feeling as well as intense sensations of emotion.

To be psychic is to train your inner senses to interpret the sensations of intuition. Our inner senses are vast and constitute a wide variety of inner interpretation when it comes to intuitive-based feelings.

Such psychic senses, or Clair senses include, but are not limited to:

Clairvoyance: The ability of psychic sight.

Clairaudience: The ability of psychic hearing.

Clairsentience: The ability of psychic touch.

Claircognisance: The ability of instantaneous knowing.

Clairempathy: The ability to sense the feelings/emotions within others.

Clairscent: The ability of psychic smell.

Clairgustance: The ability of psychic taste.

The word "clair" simply represents clear or clarity through our own inner sensing. It is very possible for any psychic/intuitive to become proficient through all of these described clair-enabled senses.

How These Senses Are Developed

As we are able to develop our own external senses proficiently as a newborn baby leading into toddler years, we are able to develop our inner psychic senses just the same. It would be similar to the idea of developing inner psychic muscles as we make our inner sensing second nature to us.

For one who would like to become more visual through clairvoyance, for example; one particular technique is the ability to imagine and focus upon simple 2-dimensional shapes within our mind's eye: squares, triangles, circles, hexagons, etc. Work on expanding and shrinking the objects as well as spinning them clockwise and counter-clockwise. You may also begin filling them with a single colour, or multiple colours. Once you are able to become strong with this method, look into trying other creative visualization methods with 3-dimensional objects and re-shaping/re-colouring their appearances. A more advanced technique would include imagining landscapes in the most vivid way you can. This would include imagining long grass swaying through a strong breeze, or watching the ocean tide crash upon the shore. The more you can feel the presence of actually being within such a landscape that represents the sensation of a lucid real-time environment, the more you will allow your mind to become strengthened with an empowered inner ability of clairvoyance. As this empowered sense becomes more in tune with your reality, phenomena interpreted through your natural intuition will utilize this medium as a communicative visual-enriched response.

Similar exercises can be utilized for the other psychic senses such as:

Hearing the sound of one's own voice internally to promote clairaudience.

Detecting scents and tastes through the imagination to promote clairgustance and clairscent.

Clearing the mind and being sensitive to the feelings of others to promote clairempathy.

Claircognisance requires a more mental discipline within one's self for it to become further nurtured. As it deals with heightened internal awareness, one must be aligned in a constant flow to become susceptible to ideas/innovations or Aha! Moments. This often requires long periods of meditation to help bring the mind into void and harmonizing with thoughts that may cause belief systems and personal boundaries so that one may frequently act upon moments of inspiration.

Increasing Depth Perception

As we become more in tune with higher frequency, we increase our ability to access greater depth within our own consciousness that broadens itself out to universal levels. An intuitive who can operate on a higher frequency of love holds the capability to see more of the larger picture when it comes to any phenomena within their reality.

This understanding can be further explained through the example of geometry:

By using the example of the square, this represents all that we are able to see as long as we exist within a confined singular perception of involvement. As long as we remain attached a situation or an outcome, we will never be able to see beyond the confines of our belief systems. This would represented singular self-perception.

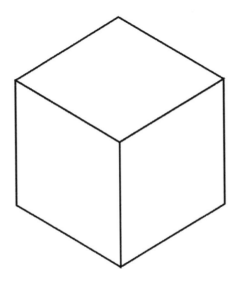

As we look into the example of the cube, this is the result of one who is able to open, trust and interpret the natural flow of universal understanding. This represents the mentality of the Rainbow Wise: one who represents expansive depth perception.

Higher frequency holds the understanding of a broader vantage point. It is not held into a perception that it is a superior position, it is only allowing us to see more of what reality contains when we learn to utilize intuition and our own psychic abilities. As we do this, our reality becomes far more vast and through operating in a state beyond attached involvement, the universe in its grand subtlety is willing to show us more beyond the standard perceptions of the physical body.

Discerning Between the Ego and Higher Mind

When one is beginning to experiment with working deeply into their own intuitive flow and inner psychic development, a common situation that may emerge may be the uncertainty of distinguishing whether the insight you are receiving is that of the personal ego or if it is of the higher mind.

As mentioned in previous chapters, the ego is not one's enemy and is not looking to be ignored, escaped from or destroyed. If you are feeling that your thoughts may seem repetitive when you are receiving conscious guidance, it's attempting to a hold a message for you: trust.

When you first begin practicing with your intuition, allow the flow of your conscious guidance to come through unfiltered. As you do this, you are in a state of pure openness where nothing is being blocked or bypassed. As this becomes more natural, you will notice that your flow will become more refined as you are no longer discriminatory in what you are willing to receive through an opened state of being.

Trust is simply attempting to look deeper into what you are openly receiving to distinguish what truly serves you beyond the thought and beyond the words. Where there is repetition of guidance, regardless if you have heard it before through anyone else, it is a reflective indication that there is something within your own conscious self that needs to be observed further. Perhaps this may involve 'trusting the process', or 'following your heart to lead you into a new journey', etc. Whatever it may be, take it into consideration despite its repetition. Your mind is attempting to tell you something. Take it to heart regardless whether you believe it is emerging from the ego or your higher mind.

True Guidance is a Current

When we are looking at the essence of true guidance, one can liken it to the current of the ocean. Upon the ocean, you are sailing upon a raft. This raft can look as beautiful or as crude as you wish as it represents your mentality of your own personal life journey.

The current represents the direction of the path of least resistance. You do not know where the current is taking you, but you realize that with no effort, the current is moving you quite quickly. But, as you look behind you, you can see the land at a great distance where you departed from. At times you may feel tired of the current not being able to share with you where it wishes to take you. Out of frustration, you pick up a paddle and attempt to force your way back to land as you grow so tired of being out upon the ocean not knowing your destination. But as we have chosen to pursue a path of our spiritual enlightenment and evolution, all the force we attempt to put into paddling simply exhausts us and we collapse upon our raft having barely moved from the power of the natural current.

This is a direct analogy of our own soul journey. There will come a time, or perhaps even many times where you will become so agitated with not being able to "know" everything relating to where your path will take you or what the "big result" may be as you continue this journey. This is reminding you that for one to follow a spiritual journey, personal humility is not a suggestion, it is a natural responsibility. You will be embarking upon situations beyond anything that the conscious self can possibly imagine. Your whole reality will transform: You will phase out old beliefs that are looking to become harmonized, transcend individuals that represented severe conditionality, transform your living and business environment and more.

The journey is very challenging. But if you realize that your life prior to your personal awakening functioned as a gauge to informing you of changes that were mandatory in being made, the journey will become a lot more smoother. Many of us feel that we want to place a great deal of guilt, grief, anger or fear on what we had experienced in the past as we are extremely critical of our own decision-making processes.

It is not about that. One who is looking to align to the essence of Rainbow Wisdom understands that no matter how dark their life gauge was representing past instances, it was all for an orchestration of divine transformation: you immerse into drama to realize how you can transcend it.

Unnatural experience contaminates each one of us so that we can eventually realize that it is time to cleanse ourselves of what has not served us, so we can feel how divine it is to move into a whole new alignment of being fully cleared and harmonized as a being of pure service.

Improving Intuitive Connection

To improve your natural intuition, this is all about maintaining a healthy daily practice. This may involve creating a sacred space within your own home that is contained with only your loving energy. Let your environment reflect vibrations that are in harmony with yourself.

- Sage your space.

- Add your favorite artwork to your space.

- Light aroma candles or incense within your space.

- Play relaxing, centering music while present or not present within your space.

- Decorate the walls with your favorite colour(s).

As your space becomes in full harmony with yourself, you will feel uplifted each time you enter it. If you notice that the energy within your space may become stale or unwelcoming, it's time to re-harmonize it with affirmations of love, or any other modality that you personally feel will enrich it into higher frequency. The key is that as long as you feel that heartfelt connection to your space every time you immerse yourself into it, this can now become your epicenter of intuitive heightening.

Meditation is a highly recommended method for broadening one's own intuitive and psychic inner senses. There are no limits to what can be achieved within this state. Whether it be to seek inner knowing, to balance energy centers within your body, or to reach a point of harmonized stillness where you enter a state of thoughtlessness.

Entering a state of void in meditation is a technique that can generate a full equilibrium of balancing the self. When you are still of thought, your body becomes absent of utilizing its own energy of conscious processing. Remaining within the void for a large amount of time can generate incredible health benefits, re-center your energy field, repair DNA and increase intelligence.

Entering a Thoughtless State

For one to achieve a thoughtless state of being while contained within their own void, it entails complete and total transcendence to all thought that you associate with. As long as we are tethered to conditions of thought, they will always continue to repeat and pull focus within our mind.

The idea is for one to see themselves as the essence of an observer. When you notice that thoughts are becoming present within your mind, simply acknowledge their existence without the need to attach to them.

Imagine that you are a rock placed in the center of a flowing pond. The rock does not attempt to block the stream, it simply allows the water to pass through it creating a relationship of symbiosis: the rock and the river are one in compliment and are never adversarial nor competitive. Look to your thoughts as rocks contained amongst a river. They do not obstruct the flow of the water, they complement it. See your thoughts as the compliment to your perspective rather than an ownership or an obligation. As you do this, the thoughts will begin to dissipate from your awareness, and through this, you will be able to enter the state of void and become entirely thoughtless.

Advanced Intuitive Methods

In the next chapter, we will look into some deeper methods on how we can adopt the flow of intuition into our daily lives through the means of developing an ability essential to the Rainbow Wise: Intuitive flowing.

CHAPTER 5

Intuitive Flowing

As we have looked more into how one can begin to encourage the connection to their intuition and gradually develop their own inner psychic senses, our next task will involve incorporating advanced practices into our daily life.

For the beginner, intuition is arranged through periodic times in accordance to schedule so that its connection can become more familiar and natural. This is where such an idea becomes transcended as we will now involve intuitive flow into every aspect of our daily endeavors.

Intuitive Conversation

When we are looking at the possibility of involving intuition into our natural state of being, this is where the archaic process of thinking about what we say now becomes passé. When we need to think about what we say or do before we do it, we only create additional processes for our mind and body to invite in clutter and distortion weakening our vital body and thought integrity process. Thinking before doing or saying in its original context was only meant to assist us in becoming familiar with our capabilities on a vocalized and motor function level. Once that is established, there is no further need to become overly logical about our inner intentions or our physicalized actions. When we continue to initiate more thought into such simplistic functions, this stems as an insecurity to ourselves as we feel we need to place a mask on our face as not to 'step outside of the norm' or not to 'rock the boat'. As long as we continue to live this way, such insecurities will only proceed to manifest within our bodies, minds and souls contaminating natural harmonized flow.

Intuitive conversation transcends the logical personality of the self. It is not absent of personality, rather; it enriches it to a purity that produces more clarity in the true heart nature of an individual.

As this book is being written, for example; no thought is constituted in the format of its arrangement of words. The words are becoming themselves as this book becomes scribed here and now. This is the understanding when it comes to natural intuitive flow. Whether you decide to have vocal conversation, or written conversation, it makes no difference as you witness the flow of the moment serving as the catalyst to your action birthing the interpretation of heart-centered expression. It is through this very fundamental that the true human being is alive and well. They flow through the alliance of heart and brain mind working in symbiosis as perceivers to the natural reception created through our subconscious funneling the unconscious creation together. This is what is known as the trinity flow:

- Conscious Self perceives the flow.

- Subconscious receives the flow.

- Unconscious is the creative flow.

Practicing the Flow of Intuitive Conversation

In this moment, let yourself open up the heart center and let that very mind share a conversation with you. It does not matter what the subject matter entails, simply allow it to express itself within your awareness. Feel free to have a piece of paper or notepad handy and a pen. Open up to the heart mind and let its expression of flow become one with your attention. Feel the focus of flow surging through your hand as you write out a conversation that the heart is sharing with you in this very moment. Let this flow happen now...

Be in reflection to what you have received and see how this intuitive flow connects with your current state of being. It is not uncommon for one to receive information that they may have heard before in some way. This is alright. Again, it's all about how this information represents guidance to you here and now.

If you feel that there was some resistance in your flow, or if you weren't able to receive anything, do not feel discouraged. You are still in the process of opening your heart up further. Ally with your feelings and as you do so, your heart will blossom like a lotus flower and you will notice an incredible transformation as you adapt more to the feeling of the heart mind.

As you continue to practice with receiving more flow from the heart mind, you will notice how incredibly vivid your reality will become. The key to receiving flow from the heart mind comes from the ability of being fully present. If you are not present, your brain mind is jumbling your awareness with thought forms that are left unresolved and are aligned with identity-based attention. Go into your stillness... enter your void... acknowledge your thoughts... become the observer... see the thoughts as presence and nothing more... rocks lying within the river bed.

As you continue to practice this understanding and enter thoughtlessness, this is what will prime you into becoming more fluidic with the flow of intuitive communication.

Vocally Communicating Intuitively

When you see someone who walks up to a stage and delivers a sensational discourse without having to use any type of script or assisted content, that person is flowing in an energy of natural conversational intuition. They are vocally communicating intuitively where their heart is wide open allowing the words to become themselves.

Yes. Our language can be as alive as ourselves. Words contain a plethora of energy behind them filled with more knowledge than some of our largest libraries on Earth. When you place these words together naturally through spoken word or written context, you are creating an orchestration of harmonized sequences that cannot only inspire and inform, but also heal. When you become adaptable to intuitive conversation, you have the ability to share a strong vibratory resonance that can be received through another to improve their vitality, transcend distortion and improve their own intelligence.

Words can function as life. If you see each sentence that you are able to convey intuitively, you can see how they shape themselves together like the body of an organism. The logical mind will never be able to understand this. Words to the mind of logic are simply contemporary language used to convey an expression through thought. Where that can be one case in point, it is not the only one. You are now seeing the usage of language through the feeling of the heart space. When you ally with words in this form of divine understanding, your whole perception of reality will function through the essence of the Rainbow Wise.

Changes in Personality

One who completely immerses themselves as the intuitive self over the identity self will begin to witness a grand transformation in how their reality is now shaped. As spoken in the Manifest Mechanics chapter relating to invitation-based reality, the invitations become answered and your whole life is now a living compliment.

Your personality becomes a living vibratory vessel where you are committing yourself to be of service through the will of your own intuition. This does not dismiss the idea of organization or planning, on the contrary; it allows spontaneous organization to take place. You gain an understanding of your life path rather than feeling that the contamination of expected organization opts you out of opportunities that can profoundly expand you further.

You are more in touch with your feelings because you are now able to listen and love yourself. As you bring these two criteria together, you are now sifting between an alignment of balanced perspective. You are more susceptible to understanding a multitude of perspectives rather than seeing only your perspective on any given situation. In the next chapter, we will look into tapping into the beauty of an infinite library where all information is contained through a collective thought matrix: the Akashic Records.

CHAPTER 6

Akashic Records: The Living Library

Rainbow wisdom stems its very essence through the spectrum of the Akashic Records. The flow that connects to our conscious perspectives operate through connecting to the strands of vibration that connects to all life and perceivable existence.

There are no words to express the infinite vastness of the Akashic Records. There is simply nothing that cannot be accessed based on the comprehension of one's own perception.

It is definition that contains us from understanding the vastness of understanding that we can house. As previously discussed, identity is looking to become transcended so that a true refined personality can be established. This personality is an interface that forms relationship and rapport with those who we interact with and the surrounding environment.

For one to understand the vastness of the Akashic Records, attempting to perceive such a reality greatly transcends our current living vehicle through its current conditioning. The idea is to transcend the idea of definition altogether. The addiction becomes the need for explanation and to discuss our experiences with all of those around us. Unfortunately, this cannot be done. What you experience in a symbiotic relationship with the universal mind has no rapport with our natural languages and comprehension. It is a vastness that cannot be normalized, nor defined, nor explained.

Our very limitation is only sanctioned on what we can understand through knowledge process. Through process comes understanding. Through understanding becomes Rainbow Wisdom.

From this concept, be mindful of your need for definition. You may experience your own perspectives that transcend beyond any perceivable explanation. Let it go. Be within the enrichment of feeling the universal mind and become immersed in the splendor of its purest sensation that you can sense.

What Exists Within the Akashic Records?

The Akashic Records represents a living library to where all life existing within the realms of causality are stored. It functions as an infinite database where all experience programming is stored within the ethers of consciousness *(Person, Place, Event, Thing).* This can be accessed by those who are able to impose the frequency of the record(s) in question through themselves generating interpretation.

The Akashic Records does not flow through the measurement of time. All is now. Its primary function is to align to the energy of an event, not a particular date. Every reality that we understand is contained within a frame that is devoid of any motion. It would be similar to looking at a photo. Through the power of our collective mind, we are shifting into countless frames of reality every second to witness the illusory experience of motion. The Akashic Records can translate event through the flow of motion, but dates are not always possible as time is merely a measurement-based convenience and does not exist within the realms of the Akashia.

One may also consider the Akashic Records to be of the universal mind, and this too would be correct. The universal mind, like the Akashic Records exists as a thought matrix consortium where all thought exists within the infinitum of existence.

Yet, there is also another branch that represents a higher extension beyond the causal/thought realms. There can be many terms for this particular branch, but some appropriate terms would be: the Akashia, the Spirit Library, Isness or Source Consciousness. This is a branch of existence that transcends all known experience, expression, causality or thought. The closest understanding is that it is purity existing beyond form and beyond measure and it completely incomprehensible.

Accessing the Akashic Records

For one to access the Akashic Records, your mind must be within a centered state of being free of the barrage of any conscious thought. This can best be achieved working within your sacred space so that you are within a heightened uplifted vibration receiving a harmonious flow of love.

One may prefer to enter meditation through this state to help them become neutralized and surrendered to intuitive flow. One may also wish to state a prayer or affirmation that reflects their loving service and for all information to be in harmony with all love and light through the One Infinite Creator. Any statement of your recognized divinity and the divinity through the one and the all is completely appropriate.

When you enter into your state of void and you feel that personal intuitive clarity, you may begin to access the records of the Akashia. You may want to begin by having a notepad and pen present with you. The first step would be to create your subject line of intent. For example:

MY FIRST LIFE ON EARTH.

This is a simple subject of intention that will allow you to tap into your record.

Next, you will begin to sense the energies that come through that subject line and create keywords based upon the intention. If we go back to the first example, we may start receiving intuitive flow that is telling us:

- KING

- PALACE

- FARMLAND

- AUSTRALIA

These keywords are branches descending from the subject line. This may be all that we can access at this time. If this is the case, do not be concerned. Everything is revealed within appropriate timing.

You may also feel that you can descend those particular keywords into sub-branches. As you discover more terms within the parent keywords, you will have created your own Akashic Record Perspective tree. As you continue to develop your sensitivity to connected deeper with the Akashic Records through your state of void, the keywords can become phrases. You may also start to receive visions that are in relationship to your subject and can document what you experience through the visions. The more you practice, the more refined your connection will become.

This exercise is but a suggestion relating to how you are able to access your own Akashic Records. Techniques are as infinite as the universe itself. Be sure to utilize practices that you feel compliment your heightened state of being. The

Akashic Records can assist in many different ways through providing you with insight into your own soul matrix, healing your own soul matrix and also offer facilitation to access the Akashic Records for another.

Accessing the Records for Others

When working with another's Akashic Records, an important principle to keep in mind is the principle of permission. Remember to respect and honour the Akashic Records, soul matrix and free will of another co-creator. This will enable integrity and your practice and will maintain a strong loving flow through your connection to the Akashic Records and a heightening state of awareness as you develop further humility through Rainbow Wisdom.

Before you offer your services as an Akashic Records facilitator for another, take the time to explore more of your own records through any practice that you see fit. The more you become familiar with your own Akashia, the more simplistic and efficient will be your journey as an observing facilitator into another's Akashia through their permission.

Healing Through the Akashic Records

If you are looking to experience healing through the Akashic Records, it is possible for one to connect to another mirror version of themselves to initiate an empowering vibratory state of healing. This is what is known as the Akashic Healing Mirror Exercise.

For this exercise, document an intention where you would like to see a mirror image of yourself that holds an assortment of qualities that you would like to bring into your present state of being. This list can be as simplistic or as detailed as you wish as you are creating a permission slip on all of the criteria that you are looking to magnetize into your awareness.

For example, one may feel that they would like to heal their current state of being by becoming more emotionally balanced. Let this be one of your criteria that you would like to have aligned. As you have this aspect within your awareness, go into a mirror and look at yourself as if this trait of emotional balance has already been achieved. Look deeply into your eyes right into your very heart and see this transformation already taking place. As you spend an appropriate amount of time on this exercise, your mind will begin propagating thoughts that are representative to the criteria you are looking to become through yourself.

The Amalgamation Effect

You are accessing different portions of parallel versions of your being and incorporating them into you through permission. As you begin to believe that these aspects are a part of your consciousness, your mind will not debate on what you hold to be true and valid. You will begin thinking as this parallel self. Through the variety of other criteria that you align into your conscious awareness, you are entering into what is known as an amalgamation effect: the ability of harmonizing multiple states of fragmented self into a whole self. We are experiencing this transformation ability on a constant basis through the people we interact with, the dreams we experience and the epiphanies we align to through realization.

The Akashic Records and the Law of Confusion

As we begin to access more of the Akashic Records, there may come a point where our intended request for information may become stagnant regarding a certain event that we are viewing. Should this happen, do not be concerned.

The Akashic Records is an expansive, infinite library where all information has the capability to be accessed, but it Is your own form of conditioning that can cause a halt in receiving information on a particular topic. This all has to do with an energetic law that we are all abiding to through our collective consciousness known as the Law of Confusion.

The Law of Confusion in its most simplistic explanation is the basis of our own free will principle. In order for one to have free will, confusion must be a constant. This is what stems us to the decision-making process of choice. As we operate within a Law of Confusion, our own perception of truth, knowledge, understanding and reality are limited to a linear stream of consciousness flow. One moment may pass where you are ultimately confused. In the next moment, a revelation may occur transcending that very confusion. It is the archetype of our self-designed linear construct that is at play here. Through this game of linear-based reality, epiphany becomes our vaccine of clarity through moments of confusion. With this being said, time, or rather; timing will become our process to understanding greater depth perception as we continue to expand ourselves to new heights of consciousness. When you are not meant to know, you will not know until another moment grants an obvious natural point of perceived clarity. Why? Because you must be of a certain vibration to understand another vibration parallel to its imprinted pattern: like attracts like.

Custodians of the Akashic Records

Through different approaches of how one chooses to access the Akashic Records, you may notice how there are other forms of consciousness that are known as the Akashic Record custodians. These very beings represent a guardianship created to keep a natural order intact through all of those who wish to expand further understandings of their own being. They operate to keep the Law of Confusion in effect as not to jeopardize entities, events and timelines. These beings operate within non-localized and non-linear realms of consciousness. Some may perceive them as lords or angels of the Akashic Records. Whether you can perceive them or not, they are there and they function as filters to ensure the integrity of the infinite thought matrix.

Different archetypes of these beings reside within our own fields as well only allowing drops of insight to come within our awareness as certain points of timing as we align in synchronicity with such epiphanies. Our own Earth also has a consortium of these beings that maintain and preserve the streams of unified thought consciousness. For any knowledge given to a majority collective before maturity can be established can be detrimental to the civilization or other civilizations that exist beyond our world in other dimensions of reality.

Entering Into Rainbow Wisdom

As you explore the thought matrix further overtime, you will see how the plethora of perspective is the very nature of how we can understand our place within the universe. As we expand ourselves further past involvement, the omnipresence of reality becomes more vivid within our awoken reality. All of our perspectives tie into experiential imprinted roots held within countless realities throughout the connected web of Creation. It is through this understanding of multi-perceptual clarity that one can access through the Akashic Records that will move you further into the Rainbow Wisdom Perception. This premise will be the discussion in our next chapter.

CHAPTER 7

~~~~~~

The Rainbow Wisdom Perception

The perception we cling to holds containment within the self through identity. As long as we continue to believe that the only perception that exists is our own, we will only condemn our expansion to the boundaries of what the self will allow.

Perception is simply known as the interface of all reality. It is how we understand what exists throughout the senses; whether physical or extra sensory. Our willfulness to understand what reality holds can be unlocked, but through the gateway of advanced heightened perception comes once again the requirement of enacting yourself through the flow of the heart.

To unlock heightened perception, one must feel in alliance towards their feelings and their emotions. Emotions are what trap us into the solid walls of a rigid self. Emotional attachment to situations prevent one from seeing beyond them. The emotions become stronger and more valued than the self as the situation seems dominant over anything in existence. This is once again a reminder of the incredible power of emotions. They exist as an extremely intense energetic.

Understanding the Power of Emotions

Let's take a look at emotions a little further. Why are they so powerful and intense? Emotions are the result of a belief system. They are a consortium of feelings stacked upon each other brought into being through our own lack of harmony with the self.

If we were to look into the feeling of fear for example: fear itself simply is a result of belief that has initiated an energetic defense to prevent one from accepting the will to change in any situation. One who is afraid cannot embrace change to transform a circumstance. The fear keeps you contained into a sense of belonging to that which you consider to be an attachment. It Is a housed energetic that has reached an extreme due to unresolved and undisciplined mentality elicited by life programming, or unnatural experience.

If we are to look at the opposite end of the spectrum representing happiness, as good as it feels; it too has been stifled by the confinement of belief. The result of the emotion reflects the satisfaction of an expectation that may have 'gone according to plan.' Happiness comes through self-satisfaction when a goal or situation has been met in favor of the one. Yet again, it houses an immense energetic of undisciplined mentality elicited by life programming, or unnatural experience.

Whether we are feeling extremely fearful or extremely happy, it does not matter as both intensities are identical.

Imagine the reading of a graph found on a Richter scale. When you are within the state of natural serenity, the line would remain flat. When an emotion appears, the line would show an intense amount of spikes similar to that of a 9.0 magnitude Earthquake.

EMOTION

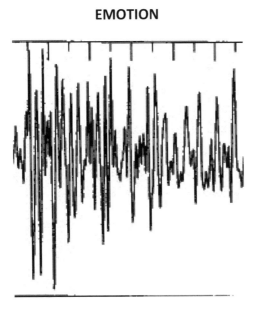

This is not to say that positive energy is detrimental. Through one who is contained heavily in negativity, positive energy exists to function as a counter-balancing energetic. And of course, it does feel wonderful to be positive. Yet, one who continues to use positive energy in overage will result in becoming confined to the situation without the ability to see beyond it just as if one were confined in negativity.

Emotions are an intense voltage of focus. Once they have been ignited, one cannot see what exists beyond the emotional attachment to the situation. For one to understand the degree of heightened perception, emotions will require balancing so that understanding can flow through.

Balancing Your Emotions

Balancing begins with the breath. When you are able to breathe in and out your stress, you are bringing your body into a state of equilibrium. When the body reaches that point, this will lead to "checking in" as shared previously.

The emotion itself is looking for its essence to be embraced. This is what has caused the emotion to form in the first place: a cluster of feeling unresolved and unacknowledged stacking together in energetic intensity.

When you are feeling the intensity of emotions that are looking to come to the surface, it is important to hold space for yourself so that the emotions themselves can be released in their unfiltered form; but through the embrace of self-clearing. Self-clearing allows you to have a space that is loving where you can bond to energies of love so that the emotion(s) may purge your being in peace.

Holding space simply represents blessing your environment as well as yourself. As you do this, the emotions released do not represent blame of the self or another person(s). They are seen in a light of acceptance and understanding so that your body may become purified from their permitted departure.

Energy Body Cleansing

As the energy body releases the entanglement of emotions, the chemical body stirs with fluctuation as the vital systems of the body re-assort themselves to a level of harmonized adjustment. This represents an energy body to physical body clearing where reception representing the chakras, meridians, nadis and psychic senses become greatly enhanced. This effect would be similar as if one were to remove oil from water. The body goes through a purification process, and as this happens, senses that once remained dormant due to emotional toxicity now become activated. Many of the Rainbow Wise are able to feel a massive shift within their own bodies after an intense emotionally releasing experience assisting them in easily exploring the greater depths of themselves through this Energy Body Cleansing effect.

Bridging into Omnipresence

Through the cleansing of the energy body with the purging of emotional release, you become far more aware of the lucid perception of reality. When one is neutral to their selves and their environment, the inner environment becomes far more prominent. The universe can now begin to communicate through you as a natural guide while you live within the physical world.

People who you encounter are now seen in an entirely new and profound way. You understand the mechanisms behind their attractions. You acknowledge the challenges they are going through, and rather than holding a determination to try to take on their challenges for them, your presence becomes the message for their healing process. You are no longer tethered to the idea that pity or remorse is the gateway to another's liberation. The understanding is that Rainbow Wisdom holds space for all to see themselves in an omnipresent view as you become a plethora of different reflections serving as a love catalyst through natural being.

One may not understand what harmony truly is until they see an example of it. It is you who can become this example of such harmony. The Rainbow Wise follow a path to where the universe guides them symbiotically. There is a lessening of conflicting decision and an increasing of balanced understanding leading to harmonized action. The natural self represents the apex of embraced service without the distortion of conditional meaning attached. You are of service because you are the epitome of omnipresence. You are adept at listening, loving and being the essence of intuition granting expansive awareness. One may see this in a larger capacity as evolving past the conditioning of self-structure. Instead, one has become the alignment of omnipresent Rainbow Wisdom.

Adapting to Collective Perception over Self Perception

As long as one sees reality only in their perception of self-meaning, the nature of the world will only become more fragmented and distorted. The key to understanding a greater perception is to align in the perception of the many. Not to the degree of agreeing or disagreeing with perceptional vantage points, but acknowledging that they exist to attain clarity of how reality is expressed collectively through its co-creators.

How can one develop themselves to adapt to collective perception? Reality is comprised entirely of vantage points from all living things. When one can see the mechanism behind all feeling through a fellow co-creator, you hold collective perception. It is where feeling is not clamored to the degree of meaning through unnatural programming, but embraced as essence as you acknowledge the beauty in expression facilitated through feeling in its purity. In other words, live for the connection of feeling without the allure to its meaning, and you will continue to digest omnipresent collective perception in wholeness.

This may sound challenging, but when one of the Rainbow Wise can transcend meaning to feeling, they understand more of the essence of reality's dynamically infinite and intelligent construct. This is your gateway to exploring a multitude of different dimensional fronts that stem through the chords of our very being. A larger picture becomes born and you are able to see reality in a beauty that can never be revealed through fragmented self-perception and definition.

Beauty through omnipresent Rainbow Wisdom therefore becomes your reality. All experiences that you personally encounter only continue to reveal true essence of your connection to all things. Regardless of the polarity through fragmented self—perception through others, you see the beauty in all singular distortions as you connect them together through the Rainbow Wisdom state. There are no longer scattered portions of colours only revealing portions of a rainbow, but your Rainbow Wisdom assists in taking fragments and piecing them together assorting them into the whole spectrum of the living collective. Through this, you are bringing forward healing even when another self cannot perceive it. You are the game master assorting the pieces of a perception-fragmented puzzle assembling a grander picture. It is through the continual growth of one who achieves Rainbow Wisdom that will bring a deeper harmony to the Earth as this lessens distortion through the collective consciousness, and increases expanded awareness for all.

When you align to this state, you are immune to the aspect of polarized encounters. You exist to assist completely in full service as you see the harmony within your wholeness of being. Whether one is distraught, or one is immensely happy, you are holding space as you digest the acknowledgement of their perspectives. It is no longer attached to you creating distorted co-creational involvement. You are flowing with the expressions, and you work to restore balance to the thoughts you encounter. Your sharing comes not from a realm of pre-conceived method or knowing, but a naturalness where intuition speaks through you as the voice of balance. As you speak, as you feel, as you breathe, you are immersed in the harmony of Rainbow Wisdom.

In retrospect, to enter a state of this nature requires a great deal of self-reflection. When one is able to fundamentally clear their entire body/mind/spirit matrix to a point where drama is no longer an attachment, this represents the highest purity of Rainbow Wisdom.

CONCLUSION

The purpose of this book is to serve you as a guide on a continual basis as you read it over and over again. It's 'straight to the point' clarity is present to provide you with "on the shelf" knowledge that will serve you through the timing that is acceptable for further clarity to be understood and taken off the shelf for you to assimilate into Rainbow Wisdom.

The encouragement given through Rainbow Wisdom is the ability for one to self-explore. As you continue to explore further in this manner, your realizations will meet a mutual relationship relating to the perspective shared within this book.

The words chosen for this book is specific to help you reach a continuance of epiphany and clarity. Its short and simple approach will enable pathways within the mind to form as you begin to experience reality anew adapting to flowing in different colour spectrums as it pertains to knowledge and understanding. The more that you understand, the more you will expand into the spectrum of the Rainbow Wise.

What is wise for you to understand is that you hold all capabilities described within this book: you are already Rainbow Wise. All it takes is the ability to strip away the layers of fog that prevent you in seeing this for yourself. As you strip those layers away, embrace those areas of confusion as they were all part of the plan in purifying your connection to clarity in ways you never thought would be possible.

Our minds are a powerful tool. And like any tool, it can be misused. For generations, our civilization has been contaminated with the validity of our own conditioning. What may seem upsetting to many is seen as a blessing to the few. For those that understand that contamination is necessary to refine our connection into a greater depth perception of love and consciousness expansion, they can be considered initiates of Rainbow Wisdom.

Remember that you are never alone in your life journey. The Rainbow Wise exist all around you and will show themselves within your reality simply upon the asking and action-taking you perform. Guidance is all around you in a variety of forms: from the synchronicity of person, places, events and objects. Listen to your reality as you ask for assistance. It translates to you through signs that may seem miniscule, but hold the answers that you are looking for if you can become aware of such subtle energies.

On behalf of the author of this book, your interest in this material is deeply appreciated. This has the opportunity to be the first of future volumes to come. Your participation and the participation of others can make this book a valuable tool for those that are looking to step into a new reality: one that allows you to bond with your greatness and achieve universal understanding through the perception of Rainbow Wisdom.

With love and appreciation,

Brad Johnson

Visit Brad Johnson's website for more information on private sessions, online training classrooms, spiritual educational products and more!

www.ConsciousMatrix.com

Made in the USA
San Bernardino, CA
05 November 2014